MICROWAVE COOKING

Editor:
Valerie Ferguson

LORENZ BOOKS

Contents

Introduction

When it was first introduced the microwave oven was the most radical innovation in the kitchen for decades. Not only did it cook food more rapidly than a conventional oven, but it could also reheat in a matter of seconds. Since then microwaves have advanced to better preserve colour, taste and texture, and improved technology means that they can now grill and brown food for additional flexibility and flavour. In the microwave additional cooking liquid is minimal, therefore fewer nutrients are lost during cooking, and because cooking times are precise little interference is needed, making it an ideal method for busy cooks. Cooking times may be reduced by up to 75 per cent, the microwave uses less energy and so cuts costs.

Almost anything, from a simple baked potato to dinner party dishes, can be cooked in the microwave, and some types of food are particularly well suited to it. Fish and seafood are ideal, as their delicate texture and flavour are preserved. Vegetables can be cooked to tender-crisp perfection with only the minimal amount of water, while cooking rice guarantees superb results every time, and no sticky pans to wash.

All About Microwaves

Understanding how this form of energy works will help you to use it efficiently and with maximum benefit.

What are Microwaves?

Microwaves are electro-magnetic waves that are reflected by some materials, such as metal, pass through some, such as glass, and are absorbed by some, such as water.

How they Work

Household electricity is converted into microwaves by a magnetron vacuum tube inside the microwave oven and the microwaves are directed into the oven cavity and stirred by a fan for even distribution. The metal lining inside the base and walls of the oven contain the microwaves within the cavity and the doors and frames of all models are fitted with special safety seals so that microwaves do not escape.

Speedy Cooking

Microwaves cook differently from conventional methods. They are absorbed by the moisture in food, causing the food molecules to vibrate rapidly – millions of times per second. This produces intense heat, which cooks the food very fast, while the container remains cool and can therefore be rotated or moved without needing oven gloves. (Dishes and plates must be microwaveproof.)

MICROWAVE POWERS
Getting used to the speed of microwave cooking does take time. Check your food often during the cooking process until you know your microwave really well. All the recipes in this book were created and tested using microwave ovens with a maximum power output of 650–700 watts. If your machine has a different wattage, consult your manufacturer's instruction booklet for information on how to adjust the cooking times for your machine.

Above: There is a wide range of foods that can be cooked quickly and with less effort and energy use in a microwave.

FOOD FACTS

The factors that affect microwave cooking differ from those that apply to conventional methods.

Starting Temperature

Foods that are cooked from room temperature will take less time to cook than frozen or chilled foods. The cooking times for the recipes given in this book are based on starting temperatures at which foods are normally stored.

Density

The denser the food, the longer it takes to cook. Potatoes, for example take longer than sponge cakes. Similarly, a dense mass of food, such as a whole cauliflower, takes longer than the same quantity divided into pieces and spread out.

Composition

Foods that are high in fats and sugars absorb microwave energy more readily than those that are high in liquids, and so cook faster. Equally, foods that are low in moisture, such as cakes, cook faster than those with a high water content, such as vegetables.

Size and Shape

Smaller pieces of food cook more quickly than larger ones and uniformly shaped pieces cook more evenly than irregular ones. If unevenly shaped food cannot be cut into regular shapes arrange it with the thinner part towards the centre of the dish. Round shapes cook more evenly than square, oval or rectangular ones. It is a good idea to wrap the corners of dishes with small pieces of smooth foil to prevent charring.

Above: Vegetables and fruit cooked in the microwave keep their colour, flavour, texture and a high proportion of their vitamin content.

Dishes & Utensils

The microwave oven enables you to use a wider range of equipment than for conventional cooking.

Special Equipment

There are many specialist innovations in microwave cookware. Several ranges manufactured from polythene, polystyrene and thermoplastics are widely available and come in a comprehensive range of sizes and shapes. A browning dish is a useful extra. Made of a glass ceramic substance with a coating that absorbs microwave energy, the dish is preheated in the microwave until the base coating changes colour – usually for about 8 minutes on HIGH, but always follow the manufacturer's instructions. Browning dishes have many applications: they are useful for burgers, chops, sausages and steaks and can also be used to "fry" eggs and sandwiches and to brown vegetables.

Above: There are now a wide range of cookware made especially for the different functions of a microwave.

Cotton and Linen

Napkins are ideal for wrapping items in for warming up briefly, such as reheating bread rolls before serving. Avoid synthetic fibres and fabrics containing a proportion of them, as they will be damaged.

Plastics

Thermoplastic materials are microwave-proof, but other plastics are likely to melt or distort, especially if used for cooking foods with a high fat or sugar content. Dishwasher-safe plastic is a good indication of suitability for the microwave. Plastic wrap for use in the microwave and items such as bags suitable for roasting or boil-in-the-bag cooking work well. Pierce a bag or film before cooking to allow steam to escape and take extra care when opening plastic bags to avoid being scalded. Replace any metal ties with elastic or string. Do not use thin polythene bags, as they will not withstand the heat of the food, although thicker storage or freezer bags are acceptable.

Glass, Pottery and China

Ovenproof and plain glass, pottery and china are all suitable. Check that containers do not have a metallic trim, screws or handles. Ovenproof glass and glass ceramic dishes are ideal, as they can go from freezer to microwave and vice versa.

Paper

Kitchen paper, paper napkins, paper cups, cartons, paper freezer wrap and the paper pulp board often used for supermarket packaging are all suitable

Above: Avoid using any of these items in the microwave oven.

when thawing, reheating or for very short cooking and for foods with a low fat, sugar or water content. Avoid wax-coated cups and plates.

Wooden and Wicker

These may be used for short periods of reheating, but wood or wicker will tend to dry out, crack or char.

Out of Bounds

Metal in any form is unsuitable for use in the microwave oven, except for small pieces of smooth foil used for shielding vulnerable areas of food. This includes foil dishes, china with a metal design, metal skewers and even paper-coated metal ties for plastic bags. Do not use unglazed earthenware. Avoid mugs and cups with glued-on handles, as these can loosen and so could cause a scald.

Left: Many items of domestic cookware can be used and often the same container can go from oven to table for serving.

Techniques

Your success in using the microwave oven will be greater if you follow these simple rules every time you cook.

Preparing Ingredients
Cut ingredients into even-size pieces so that they cook at the same rate.

• Slice vegetables into slim strips.
• Large vegetables, such as swede or potatoes, can be cut into neat cubes to promote quick, even cooking.
• Slicing meat across the grain into thin pieces helps to tenderize it.

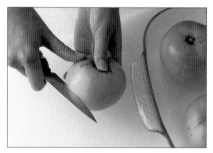

Scoring or Pricking Foods
Foods with tight skins or membranes, such as sausages, whole fish, jacket potatoes, egg yolks and apples must be lightly pricked or scored before cooking or they are liable to burst.

Stirring
In a microwave, stirring redistributes heat and cooked areas from the outside to the centre of a dish for even cooking. Precise stirring instructions are given in a recipe if it is important; if not, stirring halfway through cooking is usually sufficient to achieve a good result.

Rotating
Most modern microwaves now have a turntable, so rotating manually isn't necessary. However, you might want to keep an eye on your food to make sure it is cooking evenly, especially if you have a browning function, and turn half way through cooking.

Redistributing Food

Rearranging foods ensures even results. Move foods from the outside of the dish to the centre and vice versa.

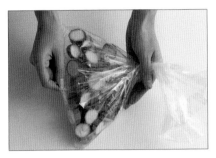

• Rearrange foods cooked in a bag by gently shaking the bag from side to side.

• Arrange whole fish in pairs, head to tail, to form an even area that will cook uniformly.
• When reheating plated meals, ensure food is spread out evenly with thicker vegetables towards the edge so that they receive the most energy.

Arranging Food

A careful arrangement of foods for microwave cooking can ensure that an ingredient is perfectly cooked.

• Try to cook foods of an even or similar size together and arrange them in a ring, leaving the centre empty.
• If foods are of an irregular shape, arrange them like spokes with the thicker sections to the outside of the dish. This will balance the cooking times of the thick and thin pieces.

• Use special plastic microwave stacking rings when reheating more than one plated meal so that they all receive an equal amount of energy and reheat uniformly.
• Try to ensure an even depth of food. Otherwise, stir or rearrange ingredients to achieve this.
• Cakes cook best in a ring mould. If you don't have one, then there is a simple method you can use. Place a glass jar in a round microwaveproof dish and hold it in place while adding the mixture.

Turning Over

Many large or dense items of food, such as potatoes or chicken drumsticks, should be turned over about halfway through cooking to ensure good results.

Shielding

Some parts of foods are vulnerable to overcooking; protect them with small smooth strips of foil. It is important that the foil does not touch the oven walls. Place it on the food for about half the cooking time, secured with wooden cocktail sticks.

Check the manufacturer's handbook to ensure that this is permissible in your oven model.

COOK'S TIP: Microwave-safe plastic wrap is the most practical choice of covering, allowing you to see what is happening in the dish. When folded back at one corner, the contents can be stirred during cooking without discarding it. Always remove the film carefully, starting at the side farthest away from you to avoid scalding your hands or bare forearms.

• Shield wing tips on poultry and the thinner tail-ends on ducks to prevent them from overcooking.
• Shield protruding bones, such as those you will find on a rack of lamb, to prevent scorching.
• Shield the narrow ends of joints of meat, such as at the end of a leg of lamb or pork.

• Protect fish heads and tails to prevent eyes from bursting and thin areas from overcooking. (If you prefer to serve fish without heads and tails, remove these before cooking.) Even though microwave cooking is a moist method, foods can dry out because of the speed with which moisture evaporates from them.

Covering and Wrapping

Problems of surfaces drying out, food splattering on the cavity walls and slower-than-optimum cooking times can all be eliminated by covering or wrapping foods. This locks in moisture, retains juices and speeds up cooking by trapping heat-retaining steam.

• Use double-strength plastic cooking bags, suitable for boiling ("boil-in-the-bag" or "cook-bags") or roasting bags for vegetables, meat and poultry. Replace metal ties with elastic bands.
• Some bags come with special, microwaveproof plastic clips.
• String can be used to tie bags loosely closed.

• Cover bowls tightly with microwave-safe plastic wrap. Puncture the top to allow steam to escape during cooking.
• Turn back a small area of plastic wrap to provide a vent. Take care when removing plastic wrap, as it will trap scalding-hot steam even if vented.
• Greaseproof paper may be used to cover small bowls, for example. Secure it with a large elastic band.

• Use a tight-fitting, purpose-made lid or improvise by using a saucer or plate. Make sure that they are microwaveproof.

• Use kitchen paper to cover potatoes and bread, as it absorbs excess moisture.
• Covering bacon with kitchen paper prevents spattering and danger of nasty burns.
• Kitchen paper is good for making dried herbs and as a base on which to stand food.
• Dampened kitchen paper can be used for reheating and steaming pancakes and shellfish.

Removing Excess Cooking Juices

Any juices that seep from food will absorb microwave energy. If there is a great quantity and the cooking time is longer than about 5 minutes on HIGH, it is advisable to remove some liquid regularly during cooking, or the excess juices could prolong the cooking time. You might find this happens when cooking chicken, duck or turkey. Liquid can always be replaced towards the end of the cooking time if you find that the food starts to dry out too much.

Standing Times

Food continues to cook by conduction after the microwave energy has been turned off. As there is residual heat, it is important to err on the safe side and undercook rather than overcook food. There is no rescue package for overcooked food, but additional cooking time can be given if the dish is still inadequately cooked after observing the standing time.

Browning Foods

Foods cooked in solo microwaves do not readily brown. Try the following tips to encourage browning or disguise any pale results.
• Grill foods such as gratins and roasts before or after microwave cooking.
• Use a microwave browning dish for chops, steaks, toasted sandwiches, stir-fries and individual chicken portions.
• Buy or make a browning mix to coat foods – paprika, toasted breadcrumbs, crushed crisps, soy sauce, Worcestershire sauce and soup mixes all work well.
• Bacon browns readily, so it can be laid over poultry or roast meat.
• Baked items, such as cakes and biscuits, can be sprinkled or coated with toasted coconut, chocolate vermicelli, roughly chopped nuts, chopped glacé fruits, seeds, such as sunflower and poppy, and dark spices.
• Glaze ham, poultry or game with fruit preserve, particularly redcurrant jelly or citrus marmalade, before cooking, to add colour. Use a broad pastry brush for even coverage.
• Add icing to a pale cake or other baked items after cooking.

Grill and Combi Ovens

Since the first microwave ovens came on the market, technical developments have seen new models become available that have a grill (broiler) function. This makes browning quick and easy, and means that the oven can also be used for grilling. A combi microwave is an all-in-one oven that provides all the features of a solo microwave, plus a grill, but also has a convection oven for baking and roasting or crisping.

The Microwave & Freezer

Microwaves defrost food both quickly and efficiently. Almost all models have a DEFROST control or button to ensure optimum action.

Defrosting Tips

Refer to the manufacturer's handbook for a guide to defrosting times. Err on the side of safety by timing for too short a period, rather than too long.
• Follow standing times as foods will continue to thaw by conduction. Defrost until just icy.
• Open cartons and remove any metal lids, ties or fastenings before defrosting.
• Before defrosting, prick, slash or vent membranes and skins. Pierce plastic wrap, pouches or similar wrappings.
• Never try to hurry the process.
• Transfer frozen foods in foil to a suitable dish for the microwave.
• Turn foods over during defrosting, halfway through the recommended time.
• If food cannot be turned, rotate it regularly for even defrosting.
• Flex and rotate pouches of food that cannot be broken up or stirred.
• Place cakes, rolls and pastry items on a double sheet of kitchen paper to absorb excess moisture.
• Break up blocks of frozen food with a fork during defrosting.
• Separate blocks of frozen meat items, such as hamburgers, as they defrost.
• Remove any juices or drips with a bulb baster or spoon.
• Defrost meat joints, whole birds and whole fish until icy, then leave to defrost completely at room temperature before cooking.

Freezer to Microwave Reminders

When freezing home-made food that will later be defrosted or cooked in the microwave, the following hints are worth noting.
• Freeze all cooked food in a microwaveproof container.
• Arrange cooked main courses on microwaveproof plates and freeze.
• Freeze soups, casseroles and hot pots in freezer bags that are also suitable for microwave defrosting.

Cook and Freeze in One Bag

1 Cook chopped up fruits such as apples and pears in a roasting bag or boilable bag.

2 When cooked, crush the fruit in the bag to make a purée and seal while still hot. As it cools it will form a vacuum pack that is ideal for freezing and ready for defrosting or reheating.

Making the Most of Your Microwave

These are just some of the cooking techniques that can be done in a matter of minutes. You will soon discover others that suit your style of cooking.

Peeling Peaches and Apricots

Place up to four peaches in a microwaveproof bowl with very little water. Cover and microwave on HIGH for 1–1½ minutes. Leave to stand for 5 minutes, then drain and peel.

Softening Butter

Microwave on HIGH for 5–10 seconds, then leave to stand for 5 minutes before using.

COOK'S TIP: Croûtons can be flavoured in a variety of ways to complement the dishes they garnish. A crushed garlic clove or a little dried oregano can be added to the butter for butter-crisp croûtons. Chopped fresh herbs, such as tarragon or parsley, should be tossed with the cooked croûtons. Grated Parmesan cheese or lemon rind can also be added to cooked croûtons.

To Make Croûtons

1 For dry, oil-free croûtons, dice 175 g/6 oz bread into cubes.

2 Place on kitchen paper on a large flat microwaveproof plate and microwave on HIGH for 3–4 minutes, stirring once every minute, until dry.

3 For butter-crisp croûtons, place 25 g/1 oz/2 tbsp butter in a microwaveproof dish and microwave on HIGH for 30 seconds to melt. Add 175 g/6 oz bread cubes and toss to coat. Microwave on HIGH for 3–4 minutes, stirring every minute, until crisp and brown. Freeze until needed (no need to defrost).

Peeling Tomatoes

Place up to six tomatoes in a ring on kitchen paper. Microwave on HIGH for 10–15 seconds. Leave to stand for 15 minutes, then peel.

To Dry Bread for Crumbs

1 Place a thick slice of bread on a microwaveproof plate and microwave on HIGH for 2½–3½ minutes.

2 When the bread is completely cool, grate it. Use at once or freeze until needed.

Garlic or Herb Bread

To serve four, cut a 115 g/4 oz French stick into diagonal slices about 4 cm/ 1½ in thick, almost to the base but not quite through. Spread garlic or herb butter between the slices and re-form the loaf. Wrap loosely in kitchen paper and microwave on HIGH for 1½ minutes. Serve at once.

Drying Herbs and Citrus Rinds

Position on a microwaveproof plate and microwave on HIGH until dry. Check at 1 minute intervals.

Proving Yeast Dough

Give a 900 g/2 lb piece of dough short bursts of microwave energy on HIGH for 5–10 seconds, with a 10 minute standing time between each burst. Repeat until the dough has risen to double its size.

Blanching Almonds

Place 250 ml/8 fl oz/1 cup water in a jug. Microwave on HIGH for 2½ minutes, until boiling. Add the almonds and microwave for 30 seconds. Drain and slip off the skins.

Toasting Nuts

Place the nuts in a browning dish and microwave on HIGH for 4–5 minutes, stirring each minute. For a lighter result, cook them in an ordinary microwaveproof dish. For desiccated coconut, spread 115 g/4 oz/1¼ cups on a plate and microwave on HIGH for 5–6 minutes, stirring every minute.

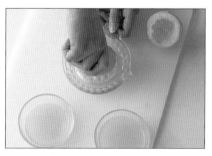

Squeezing Citrus Juice

To extract the maximum amount of juice from the fruit, prick the skins and then microwave on HIGH for about 5–10 seconds.

Defrosting Frozen Pastry

Place a 400 g/14 oz packet of pastry on a microwaveproof plate and microwave on DEFROST for 4–4½ minutes, turning over once. Leave to stand for 5 minutes before using.

Softening Jams and Spreads

Remove lids and any metal trims or transfer the jam to a microwaveproof dish. Microwave on HIGH for about 5–10 seconds per 450 g/1 lb.

Dissolving Gelatine

1 Sprinkle the gelatine over cold water and leave to stand in a cool place until spongy.

2 Microwave the gelatine on HIGH for 30 seconds, until clear and completely dissolved.

To Make Jelly

1 Break up a 130 g/4½ oz jelly tablet and place in a microwaveproof bowl or jug with 150 ml/¼ pint/⅔ cup water.

2 Microwave the jelly on HIGH for 2 minutes. Stir well to dissolve, then make up with cold water according to the packet instructions.

Clarifying Crystallized Honey

Remove the lid and any metal trims on the jar, and then microwave on HIGH for 1–2 minutes. Stir the honey well. To make clear honey more runny, microwave on DEFROST for 30–50 seconds.

Melting Chocolate

Break chocolate into pieces and place in a microwaveproof bowl. Microwave on HIGH, for about 1 minute per 25 g/1 oz.

Softening Ice Cream

Microwave about 1 litre/1¾ pints/ 4 cups hard (not soft scoop) ice cream on MEDIUM for 45–90 seconds. Leave to stand for 1–2 minutes before scooping into serving dishes.

Quick Soaking of Dried Beans

Place the dried beans in a microwaveproof bowl and cover them with boiling water. Cover and microwave on HIGH for 5 minutes. Leave to stand for 1½ hours, then drain, rinse and cook the beans.

To Heat Milk for Drinks

Milk for café au lait, hot chocolate or other beverages can be heated very quickly. Place 300 ml/½ pint/1¼ cups milk in a microwaveproof jug and microwave on HIGH for 2–2½ minutes. Whisk until frothy.

To Make Mulled Wine

1 Mix 750 ml/1¼ pints/3 cups red wine, 12 cloves, 2 small cinnamon sticks, the grated rind and juice of 1 large orange and 1 lemon, and 30-45ml/2-3 tbsp brown sugar in a microwaveproof bowl or jug.

2 Microwave on HIGH for about 5 minutes, or until almost boiling. Add extra sugar to taste, if liked, and serve the wine warm. This serves about six.

To Soften Chilled Hard Cheeses

Place about 225g/8oz chilled hard cheese on a microwaveproof serving plate and microwave on LOW for 30–35 seconds, turning over after half the time. Leave to stand for 5 minutes before serving.

To Ripen Semi-soft Cheese

Place about 225g/8oz semi-soft cheese on a microwaveproof serving dish and microwave on LOW for 15–45 seconds depending upon degree of ripeness. Check constantly and turn over after half of the time. Leave to stand for 5 minutes before serving.

Toasting Coconut

Spread 115g/4oz/1 cup dessiccated coconut on a microwaveproof plate. Microwave on HIGH for 5–6 minutes, stirring every 1 minute.

Flambéing with Alcohol

Heat the alcohol, such as brandy, in a microwaveproof and flameproof jug on HIGH for 15 seconds. It will then ignite more easily ready for pouring over the Christmas pudding.

To Cook Poppadoms

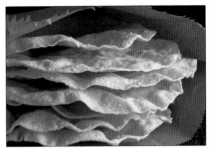

1 Arrange two or three plain or spiced poppadomson the base of the cooker or on the turntable so that they do not touch or overlap. Microwave on HIGH for 45–60 seconds untili puffy and bubbling. Leave to stand on a wire rack for 15 seconds to crisp.

2 To make poppadom cases or cups, position a poppadom over a small microwaveproof bowl and microwave on HIGH for 20–25 seconds. As it cooks, the poppadom will droop in folds over the bowl to make a cup shape. Leave to stand for about 15 seconds to crisp before removing the bowl.

To Dry Bread for Crumbs

Place a thick slice or portion of bread on a microwaveproof plate and microwave on HIGH for 2½–3½ minutes, until dry. Allow the bread to cool completely before crumbling or grating it for use

Foods Not for the Microwave

The following foods, and methods of cooking, are not suitable for the microwave and they are best avoided. You will find, however, that reheating any of these foods is fine.

Batter-based & Some Air-incorporated Recipes

Items such as Yorkshire pudding, soufflé, pancakes, choux pastry, batter-coated fish and whisked sponge mixtures need conventional cooking methods to become sufficiently crisp and firm. The microwave can be used, to make the sauce for a soufflé, and will reheat cooked pancakes perfectly.

Meringues

These should be cooked in the conventional oven since they do not dry sufficiently or become crisp in the microwave.

Eggs in Shells

These are liable to explode owing to the build-up of pressure within the shell. Eggs can however be baked, scrambled, poached and "fried" in the microwave with superb results. The membrane surrounding a whole yolk should be pierced with the tip of a sharp knife.

Popcorn

This has proved to be too dry to attract microwave energy, although some manufacturers have produced microwave popcorn, sold in a special bag with seasonings and flavourings, which works superbly. A special microwave popcorn machine can also be purchased to cook ordinary popcorn in the microwave.

Liquid in Bottles & Pots

Check that bottles do not have necks that are too narrow to allow sufficient steam to escape, as built-up pressure may cause them to shatter. Similarly, tall coffee pots with slim spouts can break or cause hot coffee to spurt out.

Deep-fat Frying

This is not recommended as it requires prolonged heating. It is also difficult to control the temperature of the fat and the food may burn.

Below: Storebought packs of flavoured popcorn work well in the microwave.

Basic Recipes

The microwave is invaluable for cooking a range of basic recipes and sauces in particular, because they complement so many dishes.

Hollandaise Sauce

1 Place 115 g/4 oz/½ cup butter in a large microwaveproof jug and microwave on HIGH for 1½ minutes until melted. Whisk in 45 ml/3 tbsp lemon juice, 2 egg yolks, a pinch of mustard powder and salt and pepper to taste.

2 Microwave on MEDIUM for 1 minute, whisk and serve. This sauce is delicious with poached salmon or cooked asparagus. Serves 4–6.

White Pouring Sauce

1 Place 25 g/1 oz/2 tbsp butter in a microwaveproof jug and microwave on HIGH for 30–60 seconds, until melted.

2 Stir in 25 g/1 oz/¼ cup plain (all-purpose) flour and 300 ml/½ pint/1¼ cups milk. Microwave on HIGH for 3½–4 minutes, stirring or whisking every minute, until smooth, boiling and thickened. Season to taste and serve. Makes 300 ml/½ pint/1¼ cups.

Variations

One-stage Sauce: place the flour and butter in a microwaveproof jug, then add the milk and whisk lightly. Microwave on HIGH as for step 2 of White Pouring Sauce.

Caper Sauce: add 15 ml/1 tbsp drained capers and 5 ml/1 tsp vinegar from the jar of capers or lemon juice to the cooked sauce. Good with cooked lamb.

Cheese Sauce: add 50–115 g/2–4 oz/½-1 cup grated cheese, a pinch of dry mustard powder and a pinch of cayenne pepper to the cooked sauce. Whisk or stir well. Serve with vegetables, eggs, fish or pasta.

Parsley Sauce: add 15–30 ml/ 1–2 tbsp chopped fresh parsley and a squeeze of lemon juice (optional) to the cooked sauce and whisk or stir well. Serve with fish, ham or bacon and vegetables.

Jacket Potatoes

1 Scrub and prick the potatoes. Place on a double thickness of kitchen paper. If cooking more than two potatoes, arrange them in a ring.

2 Microwave on HIGH for the time given, turning over halfway through. Leave to stand for 3–4 minutes.

3 The potatoes may be cut in half and the flesh forked up or mashed, then replaced in the shells, topped with cheese or butter and heated for a few seconds in the microwave to melt the butter or cheese before serving.

Cooking Times for Jacket Potatoes	
1 x 175 g/6 oz potato	4–6 minutes
2 x 175 g/6 oz potatoes	6–8 minutes
3 x 175 g/6 oz potatoes	8–12 minutes
4 x 175 g/6 oz potatoes	12–15 minutes

Giblet Stock for Gravy

1 Place the giblets from a chicken, turkey or duck in a microwaveproof bowl with 300 ml/½ pint/1¼ cups boiling water and a few sliced seasoning vegetables, such as carrots, celery and onion.

2 Microwave the mixture on HIGH for 7–10 minutes. Strain and use the gravy as required.

Scrambled Eggs

Easy to do, and easy to wash up.

1 Place 15 g/½ oz/1 tbsp butter in a microwaveproof jug or bowl and microwave on HIGH for about 30 seconds to melt.

2 Beat 4 eggs with 30 ml/2 tbsp semi-skimmed or whole milk and salt and freshly ground black pepper to taste. Add to the melted butter and microwave on HIGH for 1¼ minutes. Briefly stir or whisk the set pieces of egg from the outside of the bowl or jug to the centre.

3 Microwave on HIGH for a further 1¼–1¾ minutes, stirring or whisking twice. When about three-quarters cooked, there is still a significant amount of runny egg, as shown here. When they are cooked, the eggs are moist, not completely set. Leave to stand for 1–2 minutes, by which time the eggs will be set ready for serving. Serves 2.

Italian Fish Soup

Microwaves might have been invented for cooking fish, as the delicate texture of the flesh benefits from quick cooking.

Serves 4

INGREDIENTS
30 ml/2 tbsp olive oil
1 onion, thinly sliced
a few saffron threads
5 ml/1 tsp dried thyme
pinch of cayenne pepper
2 garlic cloves, finely chopped
2 x 400 g/14 oz cans tomatoes, drained
   and chopped
175 ml/6 fl oz/¾ cup dry white wine
1.85 litres/3¼ pints/8 cups hot fish stock
350 g/12 oz white fish fillets, skinned and
   cut into pieces
450 g/1 lb monkfish, cut into pieces
450 g/1 lb live mussels, scrubbed and
   debearded
225 g/8 oz prepared small squid, cut
   into rings
30 ml/2 tbsp chopped fresh parsley
salt and freshly ground black pepper
warm, crusty bread, to serve

1 Place the olive oil in a large microwaveproof bowl. Stir in the onion, saffron, thyme and cayenne pepper and season with salt to taste. Microwave on HIGH for 3 minutes, until soft. Add the garlic and then microwave on HIGH for 1 minute.

2 Stir in the tomatoes, wine and fish stock. Cover and microwave on HIGH for 10 minutes, stirring halfway through the cooking time.

3 Add the white fish fillet and monkfish pieces. Cover and microwave on HIGH for 2 minutes, stirring once.

4 Stir in the mussels and squid. Cover and microwave on HIGH for 2-3 minutes, stirring once. Stir in the parsley and season with salt and pepper to taste.

5 Ladle into warmed soup bowls and serve with warm, crusty bread.

COOK'S TIP: Discard any mussels with broken shells and any that do not shut immediately when sharply tapped with the back of a knife. All the mussels should open during cooking. Discard any that remain closed.

Artichoke & Mushroom Soup

Serves 4

INGREDIENTS
30–60 ml/2–4 tbsp butter
115 g/4 oz/scant 2 cups sliced mushrooms
2 onions, chopped
450 g/1 lb Jerusalem artichokes, peeled and sliced
300 ml/½ pint/1¼ cups hot vegetable stock
300 ml/½ pint/1¼ cups whole milk
salt and freshly ground black pepper

1 Place the butter and mushrooms in a microwaveproof bowl. Cover and microwave on HIGH for 2 minutes. Using a slotted spoon, transfer the mushrooms to a plate. Add the onions and artichokes to the bowl. Cover and microwave on HIGH for 8 minutes, stirring halfway through cooking.

2 Add the vegetable stock to the bowl and microwave on HIGH for a further 5 minutes, until the artichokes are soft, then season to taste.

3 Process the soup in a blender or food processor, adding the milk slowly. Return to the bowl. Stir in the mushrooms. Microwave on HIGH for 2–3 minutes to reheat before serving.

Right: Artichoke & Mushroom Soup (top); Tomato & Red Pepper Soup

Tomato & Red Pepper Soup

Serves 4

INGREDIENTS
5 large tomatoes
30–60 ml/2–4 tbsp olive oil
1 onion, chopped
450 g/1 lb thinly sliced red (bell) peppers
30 ml/2 tbsp tomato purée (paste)
pinch of sugar
475 ml/16fl oz/2 cups hot vegetable stock
60 ml/4 tbsp soured cream (optional)
salt and freshly ground black pepper
chopped fresh dill, to garnish

1 Peel the tomatoes by plunging them into boiling water for 30 seconds. Chop the flesh and reserve any juice.

2 Place half the olive oil in a microwaveproof bowl with the onion. Microwave on HIGH for 2 minutes, stirring once. Add the peppers and the remaining oil, mixing well. Cover and microwave on HIGH for 5 minutes, stirring halfway through cooking.

3 Stir in the tomatoes, tomato purée, seasoning, sugar and a little stock. Cover and microwave on HIGH for 4 minutes, stirring halfway through.

4 Stir in the remaining stock and process. Season. Pour into bowls, swirl in the soured cream, if using, and garnish.

Chicken Liver & Marsala Pâté

This pâté is quick and simple to make, and has a delicious flavour.

Serves 4

INGREDIENTS
350 g/12 oz chicken livers, thawed
    if frozen
225 g/8 oz/1 cup butter, softened
2 garlic cloves, crushed
15 ml/1 tbsp Marsala
5 ml/1 tsp chopped fresh sage
salt and freshly ground black pepper
8 sage leaves, to garnish
thin toast, to serve

1 Trim any membranes and sinew
from the livers, then rinse and pat dry
with kitchen paper. Place 25 g/1 oz/
2 tbsp of the butter in a microwaveproof bowl with the chicken livers
and the garlic. Cover loosely.

2 Microwave on HIGH for about 4
minutes, or until the livers are firm,
but pink in the middle, stirring twice.

3 Transfer the livers to a blender or
food processor. Add the Marsala and
chopped sage, and season well.

4 Microwave 150 g/5 oz/10 tbsp of
the butter in a bowl on HIGH for 1½
minutes to melt. Pour on to the livers
and process until smooth.

5 Spoon the pâté into four individual
pots and smooth the surface. Place the
remaining butter in the microwave on
HIGH for 1 minute and pour over the
pâtés. Garnish with sage leaves and
chill until set. Serve with triangles of
thin toast.

Eggs en Cocotte

A classic starter, these baked eggs are cooked on a base of ratatouille.

Serves 4

INGREDIENTS
4 eggs
20 ml/4 tsp freshly grated Parmesan cheese
chopped fresh parsley, to garnish

FOR THE RATATOUILLE
15 ml/1 tbsp olive oil
1 onion, finely chopped
1 garlic clove, crushed
2 courgettes (zucchini), diced
1 small red (bell) pepper, seeded and diced
400 g/14 oz can chopped tomatoes with basil
salt and freshly ground black pepper

1 Place the oil in a microwaveproof bowl. Add the onion, garlic, courgettes and red pepper and microwave on HIGH for 3–4 minutes, stirring once.

2 Stir in the tomatoes, with salt and pepper to taste, and microwave on HIGH for 3–4 minutes, stirring once.

3 Divide the ratatouille among four individual microwaveproof dishes or large ramekins, each with a capacity of about 300 ml/½ pint/1¼ cups. Make a small hollow in the centre of each portion of ratatouille and carefully break in an egg.

4 Season each cocotte with freshly ground black pepper and sprinkle with the Parmesan cheese. Gently prick each yolk with a needle or wooden cocktail stick. Microwave on HIGH for 4–6 minutes, or until the eggs are just set. Sprinkle with fresh parsley and serve at once.

Tuna & Mixed Vegetable Pasta

Serves 4

INGREDIENTS
30 ml/2 tbsp olive oil
175 g/6 oz/2½ cups sliced button (white) mushrooms
1 garlic clove, crushed
½ red (bell) pepper, seeded and chopped
15 ml/1 tbsp tomato purée (paste)
300 ml/½ pint/1¼ cups tomato juice
115 g/4 oz frozen peas
15–30 ml/1–2 tbsp drained pickled green peppercorns, crushed
275 g/10 oz/2½ cups dried pasta shapes
200 g/7 oz can tuna chunks in brine, drained
6 spring onions (scallions), sliced diagonally

1 Place the oil in a microwaveproof bowl with the mushrooms, garlic and red pepper. Cover and microwave on HIGH for 4 minutes, stirring halfway through cooking. Stir in the tomato purée, then add the tomato juice, peas and crushed peppercorns to taste. Cover the bowl and microwave on HIGH for a further 4 minutes, stirring halfway through cooking.

2 Bring a large pan of lightly salted water to the boil and cook the pasta for 10–12 minutes. When the pasta is almost ready, add the tuna to the sauce and microwave on HIGH for 1 minute. Stir in the spring onions. Drain the pasta and transfer to a bowl. Pour over the sauce, toss and serve.

Sweet-&-sour Fish

Serves 4

INGREDIENTS
60 ml/4 tbsp cider vinegar
45 ml/3 tbsp light soy sauce
50 g/2 oz/¼ cup white sugar
15 ml/1 tbsp tomato purée (paste)
25 ml/5 tsp cornflour (cornstarch)
250 ml/8 fl oz/1 cup water
1 green (bell) pepper, seeded and sliced
225 g/8 oz can pineapple pieces in fruit juice
225 g/8 oz tomatoes, peeled and chopped
225 g/8 oz/3¼ cups sliced button (white) mushrooms
675 g/1½ lb chunky haddock fillets, skinned
salt and freshly ground black pepper

1 Mix the vinegar, soy sauce, sugar and tomato purée in a microwaveproof bowl. Blend the cornflour and water to a smooth paste with water, then add to the bowl, stirring well. Microwave on HIGH for 2–2½ minutes, stirring three times, until smooth, boiling and thickened.

2 Add the remaining ingredients, except the fish and microwave on HIGH for 2 minutes, stirring halfway through. Season, then place the fish in a single layer in a microwaveproof dish and pour over the sauce. Cover and microwave on HIGH for 8–10 minutes. Leave to stand for 5 minutes.

Right: Tuna & Mixed Vegetable Pasta (top); Sweet-&-sour Fish

Mediterranean Plaice

Sun-dried tomatoes, toasted pine nuts and anchovies make a flavoursome combination for the stuffing mixture.

Serves 4

INGREDIENTS
4 plaice fillets, about 225 g/8 oz each,
    skinned
75 g/3 oz/6 tbsp butter
1 small onion, chopped
1 celery stick, finely chopped
115 g/4 oz/2 cups fresh white breadcrumbs
45 ml/3 tbsp chopped fresh parsley
30 ml/2 tbsp pine nuts, toasted
3–4 pieces sun-dried tomatoes in oil,
    drained and chopped
50 g/2 oz can anchovy fillets, drained
    and chopped
75 ml/5 tbsp fish stock
freshly ground black pepper

1 Using a sharp knife, cut the plaice fillets in half lengthways to make eight smaller fillets.

2 Place the butter in a microwave-proof bowl and add the onion and celery. Cover and then microwave on HIGH for 2 minutes, stirring halfway through cooking.

3 Mix together the breadcrumbs, parsley, pine nuts, sun-dried tomatoes and anchovies. Stir in the softened vegetables with their buttery juices and season with pepper.

4 Divide the stuffing into eight portions. Taking one portion at a time, form the stuffing into balls, then roll up each one inside a plaice fillet. Secure the rolls with wooden cocktail sticks.

5 Place the rolled fillets in a buttered microwaveproof dish. Pour in the stock and cover the dish. Microwave on HIGH for 6–8 minutes, or until the fish flakes easily. Remove the cocktail sticks. Transfer the fish to a heated serving dish using a slotted spoon.

6 Sprinkle with a little extra parsley if you have it and then serve with a little of the cooking juices drizzled over.

Ginger Prawns

Serves 4

INGREDIENTS
225 g/8 oz raw tiger prawns (jumbo shrimp),
    peeled
⅓ cucumber
15 ml/1 tbsp sunflower oil
15 ml/1 tbsp sesame seed oil
175 g/6 oz mangetouts (snow peas), trimmed
4 spring onions (scallions), sliced diagonally
chopped fresh coriander (cilantro), to garnish

FOR THE MARINADE
15 ml/1 tbsp clear honey
15 ml/1 tbsp light soy sauce
15 ml/1 tbsp dry sherry
2 garlic cloves, crushed
small piece of fresh root ginger, chopped
juice of 1 lime

1 Combine the marinade ingredients,
stir in the prawns and marinate for
1–2 hours. Slice the cucumber in half
lengthways, scoop out the seeds, then
slice each half into crescents. Set aside.

2 Place the oils in a large microwaveproof bowl. Microwave on HIGH for
30 seconds. Drain the prawns (reserving
the marinade) and add them to the oils.
Cover and microwave on HIGH for
1½–2½ minutes, stirring halfway through
cooking, until they begin to turn pink.

3 Add the mangetouts, cucumber and
marinade, cover and microwave on
HIGH for 1–2 minutes. Stir in the
spring onions, garnish and serve.

Provençal Fish

Serves 4

INGREDIENTS
4 white fish cutlets, about 150 g/5 oz each
45 ml/3 tbsp fish stock
45 ml/3 tbsp dry white wine
1 bay leaf, a few black peppercorns and a
    strip of pared lemon zest, for flavouring
sprigs fresh parsley, to garnish

FOR THE TOMATO SAUCE
400 g/14 oz can chopped tomatoes
1 garlic clove, crushed
15 ml/1 tbsp sun-dried tomato paste
15 ml/1 tbsp pastis
15 ml/1 tbsp drained capers
12–16 black olives, stoned
salt and freshly ground black pepper

1 Place all the tomato sauce
ingredients in a microwaveproof bowl.
Cover and microwave on HIGH for
4–6 minutes, stirring twice.

2 Place the white fish cutlets in a
microwaveproof dish, pour over the
stock and wine and add all the
flavourings. Cover and microwave on
HIGH for 5 minutes, rotating the dish
twice. Leave to stand for 2 minutes.

3 Using a slotted spoon, transfer the
fish to a heated dish. Strain the stock
into the tomato sauce and mix well.
Season the sauce, pour it over the fish
and serve, garnished with parsley.

Right: Ginger Prawns (top); Provençal Fish

Hot Chilli Chicken

A lovely deep-flavoured dish that tastes like it's been simmered for hours.

Serves 4

INGREDIENTS
30 ml/2 tbsp tomato purée (paste)
2 garlic cloves, roughly chopped
2 fresh green chillies, roughly chopped
2.5 ml/½ tsp salt
1.5 ml/¼ tsp sugar
5 ml/1 tsp chilli powder
2.5 ml/½ tsp paprika
15 ml/1 tbsp curry paste
30 ml/2 tbsp oil
2.5 ml/½ tsp cumin seeds
1 onion, finely chopped
5 ml/1 tsp ground coriander
5 ml/1 tsp ground cumin
1.5 ml/¼ tsp ground turmeric
400 g/14 oz can chopped tomatoes
8 chicken thighs, skinned
5 ml/1 tsp garam masala
naan bread and natural yogurt, to serve

1 Process the tomato purée, garlic, green chillies, salt, sugar, chilli powder, paprika and curry paste to a smooth paste in a food processor or blender.

2 Place the oil in a large microwave-proof bowl with the cumin seeds and onion, cover and microwave on HIGH for 3 minutes. Stir in the chilli paste.

3 Cover and microwave on HIGH for 1½ minutes, then mix in the remaining spices, tomatoes and 150 ml/¼ pint/⅔ cup water. Cover and cook on HIGH for 3 minutes.

4 Add the chicken and garam masala. Cover and microwave on HIGH for 18–22 minutes, stirring twice, until the chicken is tender. Serve with warmed naan bread and yogurt.

Beef & Mushroom Burgers

It's worth making your own burgers for the superior flavour.

Serves 4

INGREDIENTS

1 small onion, chopped
150 g/5 oz/2 cups button (white) mushrooms
450 g/1 lb/4 cups lean minced (ground) beef
50 g/2 oz/1 cup fresh wholemeal breadcrumbs
5 ml/1 tsp dried mixed herbs
15 ml/1 tbsp tomato purée (paste)
flour, for shaping
salt and freshly ground black pepper
relish, lettuce, cherry tomatoes and burger
    buns or pitta bread, to serve

1 Process the onion and mushrooms in a food processor until finely chopped. Add the beef, breadcrumbs, herbs, tomato purée and seasoning. Process for a few seconds, until the mixture binds together but still has some texture.

2 Divide the mixture into four, then press into burger shapes with lightly floured hands.

3 To cook, place the burgers on a microwaveproof roasting rack and microwave, uncovered, for 6–7 minutes, turning over once. Leave to stand for 2–3 minutes. Alternatively, for a browner and crisper result, preheat a microwave browning dish according to the manufacturer's instructions. Add the burgers, pressing down well on to the base and microwave on HIGH for 5–5½ minutes, turning once. Leave to stand for 2–3 minutes.

4 Serve the burgers with relish, lettuce and cherry tomatoes, in burger buns or pitta bread.

Glazed Rack of Lamb

Bunches of redcurrants tied with chives provide a strong colour contrast.

Serves 4–6

INGREDIENTS
45 ml/3 tbsp redcurrant jelly
5 ml/1 tsp wholegrain mustard
2 best ends of lamb, each with 6 chops,
    trimmed of all fat
120 ml/4 fl oz/½ cup red wine
120 ml/4 fl oz/½ cup stock or water
salt and freshly ground black pepper
4–6 chives, wilted and 8–12 small bunches
    of redcurrants, to garnish

1 Place the jelly and mustard in a small microwaveproof bowl and microwave on HIGH for 1–2 minutes, stirring once, until the jelly is melted.

2 Brush the glaze over the lamb. Place the racks of lamb on a microwave roasting rack or upturned saucer in a microwaveproof shallow dish.

3 Microwave the lamb on HIGH for 18–22 minutes, or until cooked to your taste, rotating the dish and basting four times. Transfer the lamb to a warm platter, loosely cover it with foil and let it rest for 10 minutes.

4 Drain the fat from the roasting dish, leaving the sediment behind. Stir in the red wine and microwave on HIGH for 2–3 minutes.

5 Add the stock or water. Microwave on HIGH for 3–4 minutes, until reduced and slightly syrupy. Season, strain into a sauceboat and keep hot.

6 Wrap the chives around the redcurrant stems and tie in a neat knot. Carve the lamb into cutlets, spoon over a little of the sauce and garnish with the redcurrant bunches.

Chilli Con Carne

This favourite supper dish can be produced in less than half an hour.

Serves 4

INGREDIENTS
15 ml/1 tbsp oil
225 g/8 oz/2 cups minced (ground) beef
1 onion, quartered
5 ml/1 tsp chilli powder
30 ml/2 tbsp flour
30 ml/2 tbsp tomato purée (paste)
150 ml/¼ pint/⅔ cup beef stock
200 g/7 oz can chopped tomatoes
200 g/7 oz can kidney beans, rinsed
1 green (bell) pepper, seeded and chopped
15 ml/1 tbsp Worcestershire sauce
75 g/3 oz/½ cup long grain rice
salt and freshly ground black pepper
sour cream, to serve

1 Place the oil, beef, onion and chilli powder in a microwaveproof bowl.

2 Microwave on HIGH for 6–8 minutes, stirring twice. Add the flour and tomato purée and microwave on HIGH for 30 seconds (stir once).

3 Stir in the stock and tomatoes, cover and microwave on HIGH for 12–15 minutes, stirring once. Mix in the beans, green pepper and sauce. Cover and microwave on HIGH for 5–7 minutes, stirring once.

4 Place the rice in a microwave-proof bowl. Add 250 ml/8 fl oz/1 cup boiled water and a pinch of salt. Cover and microwave on HIGH for 3 minutes. Stir, re-cover and microwave on MEDIUM for 12 minutes. Leave to stand, covered, for 5 minutes. Serve with the chilli and sour cream.

Curried Lamb

Serves 4

INGREDIENTS
8 lean, boneless lamb leg steaks,
   about 500 g/1¼ lb total weight
1 onion, chopped
2 carrots, diced
1 celery stick, chopped
15 ml/1 tbsp hot curry paste
30 ml/2 tbsp tomato purée (paste)
475 ml/16 fl oz/2 cups stock
175 g/6 oz/1 cup green lentils
salt and freshly ground black pepper
boiled rice and poppadums, to serve

1 Preheat a large browning dish, add the lamb steaks, pressing them down well on the dish and microwave on HIGH for 7–8 minutes, turning over halfway through cooking. If cooked on a microwaveproof plate, they will not brown in the same way.

2 Place the onion, carrots and celery in a microwaveproof casserole. Cover and microwave on HIGH for 4 minutes, stirring once. Stir in the curry paste, tomato purée, stock and lentils. Cover and microwave on HIGH for 10–15 minutes, or until the lentils are almost cooked.

3 Add the steaks, cover and microwave on HIGH for 5–10 minutes, until tender. Season to taste, and serve with rice and poppadums.

Right: Curried Lamb (top);
Pork Casserole

Pork Casserole

Serves 4

INGREDIENTS
4 lean pork loin chops
1 onion, thinly sliced
2 yellow (bell) peppers, seeded and sliced
10 ml/2 tsp medium-hot curry powder
15 ml/1 tbsp flour
250 ml/8 fl oz/1 cup chicken stock
115 g/4 oz/½ cup ready-to-eat dried
   apricots
30 ml/2 tbsp wholegrain mustard
salt and freshly ground black pepper
new potatoes or rice, to serve

1 Preheat a large browning dish. Trim the rind and fat off the pork chops. Place them in the browning dish, pressing them down well, and microwave on HIGH for 5–6 minutes, turning halfway through cooking. If cooked on a microwaveproof plate, they will not brown in the same way.

2 Place the sliced onion and yellow peppers in a microwaveproof casserole. Cover and microwave on HIGH for 4 minutes, stirring once. Stir in the curry powder and flour.

3 Stir in the stock, then add the apricots, mustard and pork chops. Cover and microwave on HIGH for 8–10 minutes, stirring once. Leave to stand, covered, for 10 minutes. Adjust the seasoning and serve hot, with new potatoes or rice.

Sweet Vegetable Couscous

A wonderful combination of sweet vegetables and spices, this makes a substantial midweek winter dish.

Serves 4–6

INGREDIENTS
pinch of saffron threads
45 ml/3 tbsp boiling water
15 ml/1 tbsp olive oil
1 red onion, sliced
2 garlic cloves, crushed
1–2 fresh red chillies, seeded and
   finely chopped
2.5 ml/½ tsp ground ginger
2.5 ml/½ tsp ground cinnamon
400 g/14 oz can chopped tomatoes
300 ml/½ pint/1¼ cups hot vegetable
   stock or water
4 carrots, cut into 5 mm/¼ in slices
2 turnips, cut into 2 cm/¾ in cubes
450 g/1 lb sweet potatoes, cut into
   2 cm/¾ in cubes
75 g/3 oz/⅔ cup raisins
2 courgettes (zucchini), cut into 5 mm/¼ in
   slices
400 g/14 oz can chickpeas, drained
   and rinsed
45 ml/3 tbsp chopped fresh parsley
45 ml/3 tbsp chopped fresh coriander
   (cilantro) leaves
salt and freshly ground black pepper
450 g/1 lb quick-cook couscous

1 Sprinkle the saffron strands into the boiling water and then set aside for 5 minutes to infuse. This will extract the subtle flavour and the brilliant yellow-orange colour.

2 Place the olive oil in a large microwaveproof bowl. Add the onion, garlic and chillies. Microwave on HIGH for 2 minutes, stirring halfway through cooking.

3 Add the ground ginger and cinnamon and microwave on HIGH for 1 minute.

4 Stir in the tomatoes, stock or water, infused saffron and liquid, carrots, turnips, sweet potatoes and raisins. Cover and microwave on HIGH for 15 minutes, stirring twice during the cooking time.

5 Add the courgettes, chickpeas, chopped fresh parsley and coriander, cover and microwave on HIGH for 5–8 minutes, stirring once, until the vegetables are tender. Season to taste.

6 Meanwhile, prepare the couscous following the packet instructions and serve it with the vegetables.

Risotto with Asparagus

This melt-in-the-mouth dish is a treat when asparagus is in season.

Serves 4

INGREDIENTS

30 ml/2 tbsp olive oil

1 onion, finely chopped

2 garlic cloves, crushed

225 g/8 oz/generous 1 cup Italian
  risotto rice

1.5 litres/2½ pints/6¼ cups hot vegetable
  stock

150 ml/¼ pint/⅔ cup dry white wine

225 g/8 oz asparagus spears, cut into
  2.5 cm/1 in pieces

50 g/2 oz/¼ cup butter

45 ml/3 tbsp freshly grated
  Parmesan cheese

salt and freshly ground black pepper

1 Place the oil, onion and garlic in a large microwaveproof bowl. Cover and microwave on HIGH for 3 minutes, stirring once.

2 Add the rice, stock and wine. Cover and microwave on HIGH for 7 minutes, stirring once. Stir in the asparagus, cover and microwave on HIGH for a further 6 minutes, stirring once. Leave to stand, covered, for 10 minutes.

3 Stir the butter and Parmesan into the risotto, season to taste and serve at once with salt and freshly ground black pepper. Extra Parmesan can be handed round separately, if you like.

Summer Tagliatelle

This scrumptious and satisfying pasta dish is quick and easy to prepare.

Serves 3–4

INGREDIENTS
5–6 ripe tomatoes
225 g/8 oz dried tagliatelle
1.2 litres/2 pints/5 cups boiling water
30 ml/2 tbsp olive oil
1 onion, chopped
2 celery sticks, chopped
1 garlic clove, crushed
2 courgettes (zucchini), sliced
30 ml/2 tbsp sun-dried tomato paste
salt and freshly ground black pepper
50 g/2 oz/½ cup flaked almonds, toasted,
    to serve

1 Place the tomatoes in a bowl and pour in boiling water to cover. After 30 seconds peel, then chop.

2 Place the tagliatelle in a large microwaveproof bowl with the boiling water. Microwave on HIGH for 6 minutes, stirring once. Leave to stand, covered, while cooking the sauce.

3 Place the oil in a microwaveproof bowl and add the onion, celery, garlic and courgettes. Cover and microwave on HIGH for 3–4 minutes.

4 Stir in the tomatoes and sun-dried tomato paste. Microwave on HIGH for 3–4 minutes, then add salt and pepper.

5 Drain the pasta, transfer to a warmed serving dish and add the sauce. Toss well. Serve, scattered with toasted almonds.

Cauliflower Cheese

Serves 4

INGREDIENTS
4 baby cauliflowers
120 ml/4 fl oz/½ cup water
250 ml/8 fl oz/1 cup single (light) cream
75 g/3 oz dolcellate cheese, diced
75 g/3 oz Mozzarella cheese, diced
45 ml/3 tbsp freshly grated Parmesan cheese
freshly grated nutmeg
freshly ground black pepper
toasted breadcrumbs, to garnish

1 Place the cauliflowers floret-side down in a microwaveproof dish. Add the water, cover and microwave on HIGH for 9–11 minutes, rearranging once. Leave to stand for 3 minutes.

2 Place the cream in a small microwaveproof bowl with the cheeses. Microwave on HIGH for 2–3 minutes, stirring three times, until the cheeses have melted. Season with nutmeg and pepper.

3 Drain the cauliflowers thoroughly and place one on each of four warmed plates. Spoon a little of the cheese sauce over each cauliflower and sprinkle with toasted breadcrumbs. Serve at once.

Right: Cauliflower Cheese (top);
Vegetable Hot-pot

Vegetable Hot-pot

Serves 4

INGREDIENTS
2 onions, sliced
4 carrots, sliced
1 small swede (rutabaga), sliced
2 parsnips, sliced
3 small turnips, sliced
½ celeriac, cut into matchstick strips
2 leeks, thinly sliced
1 garlic clove, chopped
1 bay leaf, crumbled
30 ml/2 tbsp chopped fresh mixed herbs, such as parsley and thyme
300 ml/½ pint/1¼ cups vegetable stock
15 ml/1 tbsp flour
675 g/1½ lb red-skinned potatoes, scrubbed and thinly sliced
50 g/2 oz/¼ cup butter
salt and freshly ground black pepper

1 Arrange all the vegetables, except the potatoes, in layers in a large microwaveproof dish with a tight-fitting lid. Season lightly and sprinkle with the garlic, bay leaf and herbs.

2 Blend the stock into the flour and pour over the vegetables. Arrange the potatoes in overlapping layers on top. Dot with butter and cover tightly. Microwave on HIGH for 10 minutes. Reduce to MEDIUM for 25–30 minutes, or until the vegetables are tender. Remove lid and cook under a preheated hot grill until golden. Serve hot.

Lemon & Ginger Spicy Beans

A quick meal, made with canned beans. You won't need extra salt, as canned beans tend to be salted.

Serves 4

INGREDIENTS
5 cm/2 in piece fresh ginger root,
   roughly chopped
3 garlic cloves, roughly chopped
250 ml/8 fl oz/1 cup
   cold water
15 ml/1 tbsp sunflower oil
1 large onion, thinly sliced
1 fresh red chilli, seeded and
   finely chopped
1.5 ml/¼ tsp cayenne pepper
10 ml/2 tsp ground cumin
5 ml/1 tsp ground coriander
2.5 ml/½ tsp ground turmeric
30 ml/2 tbsp lemon juice
75 g/3 oz/1½ cups chopped fresh coriander
   (cilantro) leaves
400 g/14 oz can black-eyed beans (peas),
   drained and rinsed
400 g/14 oz can aduki beans, drained
   and rinsed
400 g/14 oz can haricot (navy) beans,
   drained and rinsed
freshly ground black pepper
crusty bread, to serve

COOK'S TIP: When selecting fresh ginger choose a smooth plump root and peel before use. Store and use straight from the freezer, for grating.

1 Process the ginger, garlic and 60 ml/ 4 tbsp of the cold water in a blender or food processor until smooth.

2 Place the sunflower oil in a large microwaveproof bowl with the onion and chilli. Microwave on HIGH for 3 minutes, stirring halfway through the cooking time.

3 Add the cayenne pepper, cumin, ground coriander and turmeric, and microwave on HIGH for 1 minute. Stir in the ginger and garlic paste and microwave on HIGH for 1 minute.

4 Stir in the remaining water, lemon juice and fresh coriander. Cover and microwave on HIGH for 4 minutes.

5 Add all the beans to the mixture in the bowl and stir well. Cover and microwave on HIGH for 4–6 minutes, stirring halfway through cooking. Season with pepper and serve with crusty bread.

Spring Vegetable Medley

A colourful, dazzling medley of fresh and sweet young vegetables.

Serves 4

INGREDIENTS

15 ml/1 tbsp groundnut oil
1 garlic clove, sliced
2.5 cm/1 in piece fresh ginger root, finely
  chopped
115 g/4 oz baby carrots
115 g/4 oz patty pan squash
115 g/4 oz baby sweetcorn
115 g/4 oz French beans
115 g/4 oz sugar snap (snow) peas
115 g/4 oz young asparagus, cut into
  7.5 cm/3 in pieces
8 spring onions (scallions), cut into pieces
115 g/4 oz cherry tomatoes
juice of 2 limes
15 ml/1 tbsp clear honey
15 ml/1 tbsp soy sauce
5 ml/1 tsp sesame oil

1 Place the groundnut oil in a large microwaveproof bowl. Add the garlic and ginger, and microwave on HIGH for 30 seconds. Stir in the carrots, patty pan squash, sweetcorn and beans. Cover and microwave on HIGH for 5 minutes, stirring once.

2 Add the sugar snap peas, asparagus, spring onions and cherry tomatoes. Cover and microwave on HIGH for 3–4 minutes, stirring halfway through cooking.

3 Mix the lime juice, honey, soy sauce and sesame oil together and add to the bowl. Stir well, then cover again and microwave on HIGH for 1–2 minutes, or until the vegetables are just tender but still crisp.

Mixed Mushroom Ragout

These mushrooms can be served hot or cold, and prepared in advance.

Serves 4

INGREDIENTS
1 small onion, finely chopped
1 garlic clove, crushed
5 ml/1 tsp coriander seeds, crushed
30 ml/2 tbsp red wine vinegar
15 ml/1 tbsp soy sauce
15 ml/1 tbsp dry sherry
10 ml/2 tsp tomato purée (paste)
10 ml/2 tsp soft light brown sugar
75 ml/5 tbsp hot vegetable stock
115 g/4 oz baby button (white) mushrooms
115 g/4 oz chestnut mushrooms, quartered
115 g/4 oz oyster mushrooms, sliced
salt and freshly ground black pepper
fresh coriander (cilantro) sprigs, to garnish

1 Mix the onion, garlic, coriander seeds, vinegar, soy sauce, sherry, tomato purée, sugar and stock in a large bowl.

2 Cover and microwave on HIGH for 3 minutes, stirring once. Uncover and microwave on HIGH for a further 2–3 minutes, or until the liquid has reduced by half.

3 Add the mushrooms, mixing well. Cover and microwave on HIGH for 3–4 minutes, stirring once, until tender. Remove the mushrooms with a slotted spoon to a warmed serving dish.

4 Microwave the juices on HIGH for 3–5 minutes, or until reduced to about 75 ml/5 tbsp. Season to taste with salt and pepper.

5 Allow to cool for 2–3 minutes, then pour over the mushrooms. Serve hot or well chilled, garnished with fresh coriander.

Fruity Brown Rice Salad

An Oriental-style dressing gives this colourful rice salad extra piquancy.

Serves 4–6

INGREDIENTS
4 spring onions (scallions)
115 g/4 oz/⅔ cup long grain brown rice
300 ml/½ pint/1¼ cups boiling water
1 small red (bell) pepper, seeded and diced
200 g/7 oz can sweetcorn, drained
45 ml/3 tbsp sultanas (golden raisins)
225 g/8 oz can pineapple pieces in
    fruit juice
15 ml/1 tbsp light soy sauce
15 ml/1 tbsp sunflower oil
15 ml/1 tbsp hazelnut oil
1 garlic clove, crushed
5 ml/1 tsp finely chopped fresh
    root ginger
salt and freshly ground black pepper

1 Slice the spring onions diagonally and set them aside for garnishing.

2 Place the brown rice in a large microwaveproof bowl with the boiling water and a little salt. Cover the bowl loosely and microwave on HIGH for 3 minutes. Reduce the power setting to MEDIUM and microwave for a further 25 minutes, stirring twice. Leave to stand, covered, for 5 minutes.

3 Tip the rice into a serving bowl and add the red pepper, sweetcorn and sultanas. Drain the canned pineapple pieces, reserving the juice, then toss them lightly into the rice mixture.

4 Pour the reserved juice into a clean screw-top jar. Add the soy sauce, oils, garlic and ginger. Season to taste, then shake well to combine. Pour the dressing over the salad and toss. Scatter the spring onions over the top.

Potato Salad

This colourful salad is an ideal way of making the most of new potatoes.

Serves 4

INGREDIENTS
450 g/1 lb small new potatoes, unpeeled
45 ml/3 tbsp water
1 bunch of watercress or rocket (arugula)
200 g/7 oz/1½ cups cherry tomatoes, halved
30 ml/2 tbsp pumpkin seeds
45 ml/3 tbsp crème fraîche
15 ml/1 tbsp cider vinegar
5 ml/1 tsp brown sugar
salt
paprika

COOK'S TIP: If you are preparing this salad in advance, mix the dressing in the jar and set aside. Shake the dressing again and toss it into the salad just before serving.

1 Place the potatoes and water in a microwaveproof bowl. Cover and microwave on HIGH for 7–10 minutes, stirring halfway through cooking. Leave to stand, covered, for 3 minutes, then drain and leave to cool.

2 Mix the potatoes, watercress or rocket, tomatoes and pumpkin seeds.

3 Place the crème fraîche, vinegar, sugar, salt and paprika to taste in a screw-top jar and shake well to mix. Pour over the salad just before serving.

VARIATION: To make Spinach and Potato Salad, substitute about 225 g/8 oz fresh baby spinach leaves for the watercress.

Poached Pears in Red Wine

This is an especially attractive dessert, as the wine colours the pears red.

Serves 4

INGREDIENTS

300 ml/½ pint/1¼ cups red wine
75 g/3 oz/⅓ cup caster (superfine) sugar
45 ml/3 tbsp clear honey
juice of ½ lemon
1 cinnamon stick
1 vanilla pod, split open lengthways
5 cm/2 in thinly pared strip of orange zest
1 clove
1 black peppercorn
4 firm, ripe pears
whipped cream or sour cream, to serve

1 Place the wine, sugar, honey, lemon juice, cinnamon, vanilla, orange rind, clove and peppercorn in a microwave-proof bowl that will hold the pears upright. Microwave on HIGH for 3–5 minutes, stirring three times.

2 Meanwhile, peel the pears, leaving their stems intact. Take a thin slice off the base of each pear so that it will stand neatly square and upright. Place the pears in the wine mixture, spooning it over them. Three-quarters cover the dish with plastic wrap or a lid. Microwave on HIGH for 5–6 minutes, until the pears are just tender when pierced with the tip of a knife. Turn the pears twice during cooking.

3 Carefully transfer the pears to another bowl using a slotted spoon. Microwave the poaching liquid, uncovered, on HIGH for 15–17 minutes, to reduce by half. Cool. Strain the syrup over the pears and chill. Serve the pears in individual dishes and spoon over the syrup. Serve with whipped or sour cream.

Sticky Toffee Pudding

This satisfying and warming dessert will become a winter favourite.

Serves 6

INGREDIENTS
115 g/4 oz/1 cup walnuts, chopped
175 g/6 oz/³⁄₄ cup butter
175 g/5 oz/scant 1 cup soft brown sugar
60 ml/4 tbsp single (light) cream
30 ml/2 tbsp lemon juice
2 eggs, beaten
115 g/4 oz/1 cup self-raising (self-rising)
   flour

1 Grease a 900 ml/1½ pint/3¾ cup microwaveproof pudding basin and add half the walnuts.

2 Mix 50 g/2 oz/¼ cup of the butter with 50 g/2 oz/4 tbsp of the sugar, the cream and 15 ml/1 tbsp of the lemon juice in a small microwaveproof bowl.

3 Microwave on HIGH for 1½–2 minutes, stirring once, until smooth. Pour half into the pudding basin, then swirl to coat it a little way up the sides.

4 Beat the remaining butter and sugar until light. Gradually beat in the eggs. Fold in the flour, remaining nuts and lemon juice; spoon into the bowl. Three-quarters cover the basin with plastic wrap and microwave on LOW for 7–10 minutes, until the mixture is well-risen and shrunk away from the sides of the bowl, but still wet on the surface. Leave to stand for 5 minutes.

5 Microwave the remaining sauce on HIGH for 1–1½ minutes to reheat. Unmould the pudding on to a warm plate and pour over the sauce.

Creole Bread & Butter Pudding

Sinfully rich and served with whisky-flavoured cream, this wonderful dessert is an adult version of the childhood favourite.

Serves 4–6

INGREDIENTS
4 ready-to-eat dried apricots, roughly chopped
15 ml/1 tbsp raisins
30 ml/2 tbsp sultanas (golden raisins)
15 ml/1 tbsp chopped mixed peel
1 French loaf (about 200 g/7 oz), thinly sliced
50 g/2 oz/4 tbsp butter, melted
450 ml/¾ pint/scant 2 cups whole milk
150 ml/¼ pint/⅔ cup double (heavy) cream
115 g/4 oz/½ cup caster (superfine) sugar
3 eggs
2.5 ml/½ tsp vanilla extract
30 ml/2 tbsp whisky

FOR THE CREAM
150 ml/¼ pint/⅔ cup double (heavy) cream
30 ml/2 tbsp Greek (US strained plain) yogurt
15–30 ml/1–2 tbsp whisky
15 ml/1 tbsp caster (superfine) sugar

1 Lightly butter a deep 1.5–1.75 litre/ 2½–3 pint/6¼–7½ cup microwave-proof dish that is suitable for grilling (broiling). Mix the apricots, raisins, sultanas and mixed peel, and sprinkle a little over the base of the dish. Brush both sides of the bread slices with melted butter.

2 Fill the dish with alternate layers of bread and dried fruit, finishing with a layer of bread.

3 Pour the milk and cream into a microwaveproof jug and microwave on HIGH for 3–4 minutes, or until just boiling. Meanwhile, whisk the sugar, eggs and vanilla extract together.

4 Whisk the hot milk and cream into the eggs and then strain the mixture over the bread and fruit. Sprinkle the whisky over the top. Press the bread into the milk and egg mixture, cover and leave to stand for at least 20 minutes.

5 Microwave on MEDIUM for 10–15 minutes, or until the mixture is almost set in the middle, rotating the dish four times during cooking. Place under a preheated hot grill (broiler) until golden and crisp, if liked.

6 Just before serving, mix the cream, yogurt, whisky and sugar into a small microwaveproof bowl and microwave on HIGH for 1–2 minutes, stirring once. Serve with the hot pudding.

VARIATIONS: Try using chopped dates instead of apricots. Or sprinkle freshly grated or ground nutmeg between the layers for an extra spicy flavour.

Strawberry & Hazelnut Roulade

Light-as-air, this dreamy dessert looks pretty and tastes simply wonderful, yet it is quite simple to make.

Serves 6–8

INGREDIENTS
2 large (US extra large) eggs
50 g/2 oz/¼ cup caster (superfine) sugar
50 g/2 oz/½ cup plain (all-purpose) flour, sifted twice
40 g/1½ oz shelled hazelnuts, ground
120 ml/4 fl oz/½ cup double (heavy) cream
1 egg white
175 g/6 oz/1½ cups sliced strawberries

1 Line a 28 x 18 cm/11 x 7 in shallow rectangular microwaveproof dish with lightly oiled baking parchment, leaving about 5 cm/2 in of the paper overlapping at the edges.

2 Whisk the eggs and sugar in a bowl until the mixture is very thick and has trebled in volume. Sift the flour over the egg mixture and fold it in with a metal spoon. Pour the mixture into the prepared dish, spreading it evenly.

3 Microwave the mixture on HIGH for 2½–3 minutes, until it is just firm in the centre, giving the dish a half turn once during the cooking time. Leave to stand for 3 minutes.

4 Sprinkle a sheet of greaseproof paper with the ground hazelnuts. Turn the sponge out on to the hazelnuts. Remove the lining paper.

5 Hold another piece of greaseproof paper under a tap for a few seconds to dampen it; crumple it up, spread it out again and lay it on top of the cooked sponge. Roll the cake up from one of the shorter edges, enclosing the paper. Let the cake cool completely on a wire rack.

6 Meanwhile, whip the cream until it stands in soft peaks. In another bowl, beat the egg white until stiff and fold into the cream, mixing well.

COOK'S TIP: Choose firm strawberries and slice them vertically down the centre. This will give a nice heart shape and attractive slices for decoration.

7 Unroll the sponge, remove the paper, spread the cream over the surface and dot with strawberries, reserving some for decoration. Roll up again and place on a serving plate, seam-side down. Chill for at least 1 hour, until firm enough to slice. Just before serving, trim the ends and decorate with strawberries.

Walnut Loaf

Cardamom seeds impart their distinctive aroma to this loaf. Serve spread with ricotta and honey for a delicious snack.

Makes 1 loaf

INGREDIENTS
3 eggs
75 g/3 oz/⅓ cup light muscovado sugar
120 ml/4 fl oz/½ cup sunflower oil
225 g/8 oz/2 cups wholemeal (wholewheat)
   flour
5 ml/1 tsp baking powder
5 ml/1 tsp bicarbonate of soda (baking soda)
5 ml/1 tsp ground cinnamon
3 ml/¾ tsp ground allspice
7.5 ml/1½ tsp green cardamoms, seeds
   removed and crushed
150 g/5 oz courgette (zucchini), grated
115 g/4 oz/1 cup chopped walnuts
50 g/2 oz/¼ cup sunflower seeds

1 Line the base and sides of a 900 g/ 2 lb microwaveproof loaf dish with non-stick baking paper.

2 Beat the eggs and sugar together in a large bowl and gradually add the sunflower oil.

3 Sift the flour into a separate bowl, adding the baking powder, bicarbonate of soda, cinnamon and allspice.

4 Mix the dry ingredients into the egg mixture, adding the cardamoms, courgette and walnuts. Reserve 15 ml/ 1 tbsp of the sunflower seeds, then add the rest to the mixture.

5 Spoon the mixture into the loaf dish, level the top and sprinkle with the reserved sunflower seeds.

6 Shield each end of the dish with a smooth piece of foil, shiny side in. Cover with plastic wrap and cook on HIGH for 8–9 minutes, giving the dish a quarter turn three or four times.

7 Remove the plastic wrap and foil for the last 1½ minutes, until the loaf is cooked, when a skewer inserted in the centre comes out clean. Allow to cool for 5 minutes before turning out on to a rack to cool. To colour the top brown under a preheated hot grill before serving, if you wish.

> **COMBINATION MICROWAVE:**
> This recipe is suitable for cooking in a combination microwave. Follow the oven manufacturer's timing guide for good results.

Brown Soda Bread

Nothing tastes so good as home-made bread and this speedy recipe is simplicity itself. Soda bread is best eaten on the same day it is baked.

Makes two 450 g/1 lb loaves

INGREDIENTS
450 g/1 lb/4 cups plain (all-purpose) flour
450 g/1 lb/4 cups wholemeal (wholewheat) flour, plus extra for sprinkling
10 ml/2 tsp salt
15 ml/1 tbsp bicarbonate of soda (baking soda)
20 ml/4 tsp cream of tartar
10 ml/2 tsp caster (superfine) sugar
50 g/2 oz/¼ cup butter
900 ml/1½ pints/3¾ cups buttermilk or skimmed milk

1 Sift all the dry ingredients into a large bowl, tipping any bran from the flour that remains in the sieve back into the bowl.

2 Rub the butter into the flour mixture, then add enough buttermilk or milk to make a soft dough. You may not need all of it, so add it cautiously.

3 Knead the dough lightly until smooth, then divide and shape it into two large rounds and place on lightly oiled plates. Make a deep cross in the top of each loaf. Sprinkle over a little extra wholemeal flour.

4 Cook each loaf separately. Microwave on MEDIUM for 5 minutes, give the plate a half turn and microwave on HIGH for a further 3 minutes. Brown the top under a preheated grill if liked. Allow to stand for 10 minutes, then transfer to a wire rack to cool.

Spiced Banana Muffins

Wholemeal muffins, with banana for added fibre, make a delicious, healthy treat at any time of the day. Serve them split and spread with jam.

Makes 12

INGREDIENTS

75 g/3 oz/⅔ cup wholemeal (wholewheat) flour
50 g/2 oz/½ cup plain (all-purpose) flour
10 ml/2 tsp baking powder
pinch of salt
5 ml/1 tsp mixed (apple pie) spice
40 g/1½ oz/¼ cup soft light brown sugar
50 g/2 oz/¼ cup butter
1 egg, beaten
150 ml/¼ pint/⅔ cup semi-skimmed milk
grated rind of 1 orange
1 ripe banana
20 g/¾ oz/¼ cup rolled oats
20 g/¾ oz/scant ¼ cup chopped hazelnuts

1 Sift the dry ingredients into a large bowl. Stir in the sugar.

2 Place the butter in a microwaveproof bowl and microwave on HIGH for 1 minute, until melted. Cool slightly, then beat in the egg, milk and grated orange rind. Gently fold in the dry ingredients. Mash the banana, then stir it gently into the mixture; do not overmix.

3 Half-fill 12 double-thick bun cases. Mix the oats and nuts and sprinkle over each muffin. Place six muffins in a microwaveproof muffin tray or in ramekin dishes.

4 Place in the microwave, arranging the dishes in a ring pattern. Microwave on HIGH for 2½–3 minutes, turning once. Cook the remaining six muffins. Cool on a wire rack.

Index

This edition is published by Lorenz Books,
an imprint of Anness Publishing Ltd,
108 Great Russell Street, London WC1B 3NA info@anness.com
www.annesspublishing.com; twitter: @Anness_Books

© Anness Publishing Limited 2015

If you like the images in this book and would like to investigate
using them for publishing, promotions or advertising, please visit
our website www.practicalpictures.com for more information.

Publisher: Joanna Lorenz
Editors: Valerie Ferguson & Helen Sudell
Production Controller: Pirong Wang

Recipes contributed by: Catherine Atkinson, Carol Bowen, Janet
Brinkworth, Carla Capalbo, Roz Denny, Christine France, Sarah
Gates, Shirley Gill, Judy Jackson, Manisha Kanani, Annie Nichols,
Maggie Pannell, Jenny Stacey, Hilaire Walden, Laura Washington

Photography: Karl Adamson, Edward Allwright, David
Armstrong, Steve Baxter, James Duncan, Amanda Heywood,
David Jordan, Michael Michaels

A CIP catalogue record for this book is available from the
British Library

PUBLISHER'S NOTE:
Although the advice and information in this book are believed
to be accurate and true at the time of going to press, neither the
authors nor the publisher can accept any legal responsibility or
liability for any errors or omissions that may have been made nor
for any inaccuracies or for any loss, harm or injury that comes
about from following instructions or advice in this book.

COOK'S NOTES

Bracketed terms are intended for American readers.

For all recipes, quantities are given in both metric and imperial measures and, where appropriate, in standard cups and spoons. Follow one set of measures, but not a mixture.

Standard spoon and cup measures are level. 1 tsp = 5ml, 1 tbsp = 15ml, 1 cup = 250ml/ 8fl oz. Australian standard tablespoons are 20ml. Australian readers should use 3 tsp in place of 1 tbsp for measuring small quantities.

American pints are 16fl oz/2 cups. American readers should use 20fl oz/2.5 cups in place of 1 pint when measuring liquids.

Electric oven temperatures in this book are for conventional ovens. When using a fan oven, the temperature will probably need to be reduced by about 10–20°C/20–40°F. Check with your manufacturer's instruction book for guidance.

Medium (US large) eggs are used unless otherwise stated.